RED CLOUD

SIOUX WAR CHIEF

BY VIRGINIA F. VOIGHT

ILLUSTRATED BY VICTOR MAYS

GARRARD PUBLISHING COMPANY
CHAMPAIGN, ILLINOIS

To Gladys Tantaquidgeon
with affection and admiration

Library of Congress Cataloging in Publication Data

Voight, Virginia Frances.
    Red Cloud, Sioux war chief.

    SUMMARY: A biography of the Sioux Indian who be-
came chief through bravery in battle rather than
through heredity and who tried unsuccessfully to save
his people's land.

    1. Red Cloud, Sioux chief, 1822–1909—Juvenile
literature. [1. Red Cloud, Sioux chief, 1822–1909.
2. Dakota Indians—Biography. 3. Indians of North
America—Biography] I. Mays, Victor, 1927–   ill.
II. Title.

E99.03R378   970.3 [B] [92]   74–20884
ISBN 0–8116–6611–5

Copyright © 1975 by Virginia F. Voight.

All rights reserved. Manufactured in the U.S.A.

Contents

The Oglalas

Red Cloud's people—the Bad Face band of Oglalas —were of the mighty Sioux Nation. These Indians were bold hunters, fierce warriors, and the finest horsemen ever to ride the Great Plains.

In the spring the many bands of Sioux Indians met together to perform the Sun Dance. They believed this would bring good hunting in the months to come. All summer long bands of Sioux roamed from the Big Horn Mountains to the Black Hills in search of wild buffalo herds. The buffalo provided them with food, clothing, shelter, tools, and weapons. Horses were so important in the buffalo hunt that Sioux war parties often raided neighboring tribes and captured their horses.

Celebrations were held after each successful battle. The Sioux warrior would tell of his skill in raiding for horses or his bravery in facing the enemy. Great war honors were earned for these deeds.

The Sioux brave counted his wealth in the number of horses that grazed near his tepee and his honors in the number of eagle feathers he wore in his war bonnet.

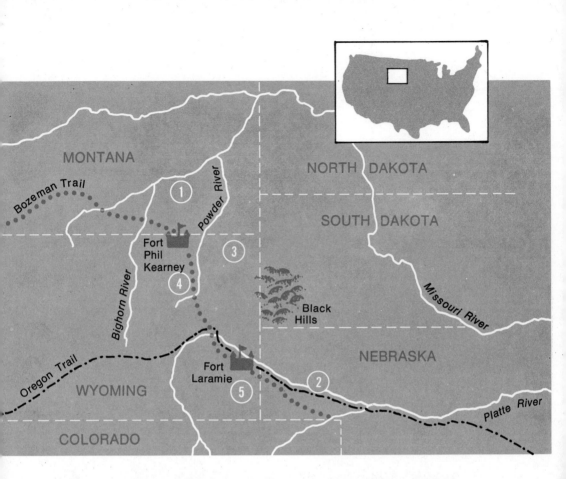

1. Powder River–Big Horn country, where Red Cloud killed a grizzly bear and earned his manhood name.

2. The Medicine Road, where Red Cloud first met white travelers going west. The white men called this the Oregon Trail.

3. The Sioux hunting grounds, where Red Cloud led war parties against the Crow Indians.

4. The Bozeman Trail, where Red Cloud's warriors fought to keep whites out of the Sioux hunting grounds.

5. Fort Laramie, where Red Cloud signed a treaty which promised that the Powder River country would belong to the Sioux forever.

1
Boyhood of a Sioux

It was a cold winter night. The wild song of hunting wolves sounded on the snow-covered plains. The circle of Oglala tepees gleamed in the starlight. Most of the Indians were asleep under their warm buffalo robes.

Suddenly a burst of fire blazed in the sky and colored the clouds red. The horses of the Oglala herd ran about in terror. The horse guards shouted in alarm. This brought the people rushing out of their tepees. They stared at the red sky in fear and wonder.

The medicine man told them not to be

afraid. "The sky-fire is a sign sent by the Great Spirit. It means that a great chief will be born into our tribe."

That same night a baby boy was born to an Oglala woman named Walks-As-She-Thinks. The baby's father laid two arrows on the child's fawn-skin blanket. He did this so that his son would grow up to be a brave hunter and warrior.

They called the baby Two Arrows. He was born in 1822, as white men count the years. His father, Lone Man, was a headman of the powerful Bad Face band of Oglala Sioux. His mother's brother Smoke was chief.

Two Arrows grew into a bright, lively little boy. One day his father tossed him onto the back of a pony.

"Hold tight to the pony's mane!" Lone Man cried. He led the horse about on the grassy prairie.

Two Arrows clung to the pony with arms and legs. The ground seemed far away, but he was not afraid.

"*Hi-yay!* Go faster!" he yelled.

Lone Man started to run. The pony began to trot. Two Arrows bounced up and down. Suddenly he fell off with a bump. He jumped to his feet, eager to ride again. Lone Man smiled because the fall had not made his son cry.

Lone Man died soon after he taught his son to ride. Not long after that, Two Arrows' mother died also. Two Arrows' heart ached with sorrow. He went alone out across the prairie to where his parents were buried in the Indian way. Wrapped in buffalo robes, they lay on high platforms.

Two Arrows laid his small bow and quiver of arrows under the platforms. They were his most prized treasures. Then he walked sadly back to the tepee of his elder sister in the Bad Face camp. He and his grandmother lived there now. But Two Arrows often saw his uncle, Smoke.

Smoke was kind to his young nephew. When Two Arrows was eight, the chief gave him a spotted pony of his own. Now he could ride often with the other boys in wild pony races across the prairie. Sometimes they would play the fight game.

"Ee-yay!" Two Arrows would swing his pony and ride hard at another boy. Yelling and struggling, they tried to push each other to the ground. The ponies squealed and reared. Shouts and shrill war cries filled the air as more boys joined in the rough game. Ponies went down. Some boys were thrown and hurt.

No matter how badly a boy was hurt, he never groaned or cried out in pain. Even the smallest boy was expected to show the courage of a Sioux warrior.

A young Oglala boy was also expected to help bring meat to the tepee. Two Arrows made himself a new bow and arrows and hunted for rabbits and prairie chickens. When he grew older, he rode with his uncle to hunt deer and antelope.

Two Arrows ran and swam to harden his muscles. He practiced with his bow until he became a dead shot. He learned to throw a lance. He became the most daring rider in the band. And he pushed himself hard to outdo his friends in the sports and games of Oglala boys.

During this time of training to be warriors, the boys also found time for mischief. Often they would hide among the wild plum trees along the river path. The girls of the band used this path to go to the river to fill water bags. It was great fun to hit them with green fruit and make them scream.

But Two Arrows was growing up. Soon teasing girls did not seem like much fun. His thoughts were on the buffalo he would hunt. He dreamed about the battles he would fight with enemy tribes. When he was thirteen, his uncle took him on his first buffalo hunt.

Most boys of his age would have been glad to kill a half-grown calf. But Two Arrows took off after one of the biggest bulls in the herd.

Holding his bow ready and guiding his pony with his knees, he raced along beside the buffalo. He let his arrow fly. It hit the bull's shoulder. With an angry bellow, the buffalo turned and charged. Two Arrows jerked his well-trained pony aside and shot again. This time it was a deadly shot.

"Well done, nephew!" shouted Chief Smoke.

Two Arrows grinned happily.

2
The Grizzly Bear

One day not long after Two Arrows' first buffalo hunt, Chief Smoke sent criers through the Bad Face camp.

"Warriors, sharpen your arrows!" they shouted. "Smoke is going on the warpath against the Crows. He invites brave men to follow him."

After the summer buffalo hunts were over, Plains Indians usually made war on one another. They would raid the camps of enemy tribes to capture horses. Or they would fight to win more hunting grounds. For years the Sioux and the Crows had been fighting over the Powder River–Big Horn country.

Two Arrows and his best friend Red Leaf went to the chief.

"Uncle," said Two Arrows, "we will join your war party."

Smoke studied the eager faces of the two tall boys. Red Leaf belonged to the Wazhaza band. His people usually camped near the Bad Faces.

"I welcome two young warriors," said the chief.

That night the two friends lay awake planning the brave deeds they would do in battle. But the next morning the chief ordered them to the rear of the war party.

"You are too young to fight Crows," he told them. "You will drive our extra horses. Brave horse guards are as important as warriors."

The boys were sadly disappointed. But

the chief had given them a task to do, and they would not fail him!

They rode around the herd to make sure that no Crows were trying to steal Sioux horses. The only enemies they saw were some big gray wolves. The wolves were trotting after the horses in hopes of pulling one down.

"*Hoka-hey!*" shouted Two Arrows.

He rode fiercely at the wolves and hurled his lance. This scattered the wolf pack. The boys bunched the horses together and kept a sharp watch as they rode on into Crow country.

Chief Smoke had sent scouts riding ahead. One day they came racing back with word of a big Crow camp. The Oglalas made camp in a hidden valley. Before sunrise, the warriors rode away. The two boys were left to guard the extra horses.

It was Two Arrows' turn to stay awake.

Suddenly he heard the scream of a frightened horse. It came from up the valley, where some of the herd had strayed. Two Arrows snatched up his weapons and ran to his spotted pony.

"Wake, Red Leaf! Danger!" he shouted.

Then he was off at a gallop.

At the head of the valley, Two Arrows saw horses running about in terror. The early light showed a grizzly bear standing over a horse it had killed. The bear lifted its huge head with a snarl.

Two Arrows' heart jumped a few beats. A grown warrior would think twice before attacking a bear this big! What chance did a lone boy and an old pony have against such a monster? Then he remembered that Smoke had trusted him to guard the horses. He gave a wild yell and threw his lance with all his might. It struck deep into the bear's chest.

The grizzly roared in pain and smashed the lance with a blow of its paw. Still roaring, it ran at the spotted pony. The grizzly's teeth and claws tore deep wounds. Two Arrows' leg was ripped from knee to ankle. The screaming pony went down and Two Arrows was thrown from its back.

Two Arrows jumped painfully to his feet. The bear had left the dead pony and was rushing toward him. The boy's heart was pounding with terror. He snatched two arrows from his quiver and shot quickly. Twang! The first arrow hit the grizzly's throat. Twang! The second arrow pierced its heart. The bear fell only a short distance away from Two Arrows.

Red Leaf rode up and threw himself off his horse. He stared at the dead grizzly. "Brother, this is a great deed that you have done!"

Plains Indians greatly respected the fierce

grizzly bear. High war honors went to a man who killed one. Only a warrior who had killed a grizzly single-handed could wear a necklace of its claws. After Two Arrows had washed his wound, he cut out the bear's four-inch claws. They would make him a proud necklace. The bearskin would make a fine robe for his grandmother's bed.

The boys heaped a mound of rocks over the dead pony, to keep the wolves away.

"Sleep well, Spotted One," Two Arrows whispered.

Smoke and his warriors returned with a large herd of fine horses that they had captured from the Crows. When the chief heard about Two Arrows' fight with the grizzly, he gave his nephew one of the best of the captured horses.

Two Arrows proudly rode his new horse back to the Bad Face camp. But his heart was sad for his old spotted pony.

3
The Young War Chief

When Two Arrows told his grandmother about the grizzly, her eyes glowed with pride.

"A fearless warrior must have a manhood name," she said. "We will talk to the medicine man about it. But first I will make a gift to give him."

She made a fine pair of moccasins with colored porcupine quills on the toes. Walking beside his grandmother, Two Arrows carried the moccasins to the tepee of the medicine man. The wise man received the gift kindly.

"My grandson has slain a great bear," the grandmother said.

The medicine man nodded. "It was a brave deed."

"He was born on the night when the red fire blazed in the sky," she continued. "Perhaps the Great Spirit sent the fire for my grandson. He has the spirit of a chief."

The medicine man studied the boy who was standing tall and straight before him. Two Arrows' strong body gave promise of what a powerful man he would one day be. His eyes, strangely light for those of an Indian, had an eagle's sharp, proud glance.

"Even older boys follow him," said the grandmother.

"Yes," the wise man replied. "Your grandson is one who was born to lead."

And he agreed that Makhpiya Luta, Red Cloud, should be the manhood name of this bold young hunter.

As Red Cloud grew older, he became famous for his courage and leadership in war. Every summer there was fighting between the Sioux and the Crows. Red Cloud was always in the front of a battle. His record of war honors grew. Other warriors were eager to follow him on raids into enemy country. He was known as a rising young war chief.

The Plains Indians counted their wealth in horses. Red Cloud captured many horses

from enemy tribes. His horse herd grew and he became a wealthy man. He gave horses away to Oglalas less fortunate than he. And when he returned from a hunt, he always shared his meat with the old ones.

The Sioux were tall, fine-looking people. Red Cloud stood taller than most. He moved with the grace and strength of a mountain lion. His neatly parted long hair framed a strong, proud face. When he walked through the camp, the girls watched him with shy admiration.

Red Cloud had eyes only for a girl called We-tamahech, or Willow Woman. She was as slender and graceful as the willows growing along prairie streams. One day Red Cloud tied four fine horses outside her father's tepee. This was a splendid gift, even from a rich man.

He waited anxiously. If We-tamahech's brother brought the horses back, it would mean that her father refused to give her to Red Cloud.

The horses were not returned, and We-tamahech became Red Cloud's wife. Most Sioux chiefs had many wives, but she would be the only one for Red Cloud during their long life together.

Red Cloud and We-tamahech had a roomy tepee of painted buffalo skins. At night on the wall behind Red Cloud's place hung his buffalo shield, his weapons, and his warbonnet of eagle feathers. Each year his war honors increased. And for every brave deed a new feather was added to his warbonnet.

Every bright morning We-tamahech proudly hung the warbonnet and shield on a rack outside the tepee. This was to show what a great warrior lived there.

Friends came to smoke their pipes at Red Cloud's fire. The precious red stone of their pipe bowls was found only in Sioux country. The Sioux thought that it was the hardened blood of a sacred buffalo. When they smoked their red-stone pipes, they felt close to the Great Spirit. Red Cloud took his pipe everywhere he went and smoked it at councils and other important times.

One day Chief Smoke sent criers through the camp.

"Take down your tepees!" they shouted. "Pack your pony-drags! We move south to hunt on the Laramie Plains!"

We-tamahech's dark eyes sparkled. "It is good, husband," she said, "that we go soon to the Laramie Plains. I want some red cloth from the white man's trading post, and some of the good medicine called coffee, and sugar, and—"

Red Cloud laughed. "Let us hope that the buffalo are many. I will need plenty of hides to trade for all the things you want."

4
Trouble on the Medicine Road

A white trader's post had stood on the Laramie River ever since Red Cloud was a little boy. The Sioux went there every year to trade their buffalo skins. This summer the Bad Face band had found good hunting on the Laramie Plains. Red Cloud, Chief Smoke, and the others came to the post with pony-drags piled high with buffalo robes. A pony-drag, or travois, was a rack made of the tepee poles. The front ends of the poles were tied on either side of a horse. The rear ends dragged on the ground. We-tamahech and the other women packed

their belongings on these pony-drags when the camp moved from place to place.

In this year of 1849, the Indians were surprised to find soldiers in blue uniforms guarding the post.

"Where are the traders?" Red Cloud asked a soldier.

"The traders have a new post a few miles down the North Platte River," the soldier replied. "The United States has bought this post. It is now an army fort."

The Bad Face band left the fort and set off down the trail they called the Medicine Road. They met some white travelers going west. At the new trading post they met other white people.

"The white travelers are going to Oregon," the trader explained to Red Cloud. "They call this road the Oregon Trail."

At first Red Cloud and the other Sioux were friendly toward the white people. They joked about the odd ways of the strangers, but they did not harm them. But soon, as more and more white people traveled on the Medicine Road, the heavy wheels of their covered wagons wore the trail ever deeper and wider. White men's horses and cattle ate up all the grass near the trail. Indian ponies were going hungry. Worst of all, white travelers brought a terrible sickness to the Plains.

Hundreds of whites and Indians died of cholera. Red Cloud hurried with the Bad Face band north to where there was clean air and pure water. Most of the band had caught the sickness.

"I will pray to the Great Spirit to show me a way to help my people," Red Cloud said to We-tamahech.

He rode into the Black Hills. These wooded hills, called Pa Sapa by the Indians, were sacred to the Sioux. Red Cloud climbed a mountain where eagles nested. He lifted his arms to the sky.

"O Great Spirit," he prayed, "take pity on my people! Show me how to save them from the white man's sickness!"

He lit his pipe and let the smoke drift upward as an offering.

The wind whispered among the trees. It carried to Red Cloud the clean, healing scent of cedar. Red Cloud took this as an answer to his prayer. He rode back to the Bad Face camp.

"Strip the bark and leaves off young cedar trees and boil them in clear water," he said to We-tamahech and the other women.

He pulled out his knife and helped with the work. They boiled the bark until they had a strong, bitter medicine. Red Cloud made everyone in the camp drink a cup of medicine every day.

From that day on no more of his people fell sick. And the ones who were sick got well.

Word of how Red Cloud had cared for his people spread to other Sioux bands.

"The Great Spirit speaks to this chief," the Sioux told one another.

Red Cloud, and many other Indians, had come to dislike, even to hate, most white people. He stayed near the trading post only long enough for his people to trade their furs. Then he moved back to wild country, far from the Medicine Road.

But a few Indians loved the fine things of the white man so much that they wanted to live near the trading post always. Chief Smoke was one of these. Some Bad Faces stayed with him, but most of the band followed Red Cloud north.

Old Smoke was still chief, but from now on Red Cloud would be the real leader of the Bad Face band. He came every summer to the post, to trade and to visit his uncle.

Trouble continued to grow between the Sioux and the white men. Gold was discovered in California. A short time later there was a rich gold strike in Montana. White people poured along the Medicine Road to reach the mines. Many of the travelers tried to bully the Indians. Some of them would shoot at an Indian on sight.

In the camps of the proud Sioux Nation, anger and hate for white people reached a boiling point. Young warriors attacked wagon trains and camps. The whites fought back. People were killed on both sides. The United States Army moved into the Sioux hunting grounds. Red Cloud and other headmen led war parties against the soldiers.

White travelers and settlers asked the government in Washington to do more to protect them. In reply Congress sent a man to make peace with the Sioux. This man was called an Indian agent.

The agent invited the Sioux to meet with him at Fort Laramie. Red Cloud did not trust the white people. He stayed away from the meeting. To the Sioux who came, the agent gave many gifts.

"These presents were sent to you by the Great Father in Washington," he told the chiefs. "In return he asks you to sign a treaty that will permit the army to build forts and roads in your country."

Some chiefs agreed to touch the agent's pen, thus giving him permission to sign their names to a treaty. They did not really understand what the treaty meant. They did not realize that they were giving away their land.

5
Chief Red Cloud

While most of the other Sioux chiefs were meeting with the agent, Red Cloud led a war party against the Crows.

·It was a thrilling sight to see the warriors ride out of the Bad Face camp. The tails of their horses were tied up with feathers to show that this was a war party. Each warrior's hair was neatly braided for war.

As war chief, Red Cloud rode in front. The eagle feathers in his warbonnet shone in the sun. He wore his special war shirt, the sign of his high rank as a warrior.

The faces of the warriors were fierce with paint. Some had painted their horses also. A few carried guns, but most were armed with lance and bow. They sang their war songs as they rode away. We-tamahech and the other women sang a Brave Heart song to speed them to victory.

The Oglala war party struck a large Crow camp and captured the horse herd. There was a desperate fight. Red Cloud charged boldly ahead of his warriors. Arrows sped toward him. He galloped up to the Crow chief and stabbed him with his lance. The brave Crow crashed to the ground.

Red Cloud flung himself from his horse and scalped his dead enemy. As he held the scalp high, a Crow arrow went right through his chest and back. He fell across the body of the Crow chief. Two of his warriors galloped close. They leaned from their horses. Strong hands caught hold of Red Cloud. Together the two horsemen carried him out of the fight.

The Oglala warriors were sure that Red Cloud was dying. They cut the arrow out of the ugly wound. Then they made a pony-drag and took him home.

Red Cloud was indeed close to death. But with healing herbs We-tamahech nursed him back to health.

One day Red Leaf came to see his friend. He told Red Cloud what had happened at Fort Laramie.

Red Cloud frowned. "It is a bad thing the chiefs did when they touched the pen," he said. "I will not be bound by this treaty. I will fight to keep the white men out of our land."

There were other chiefs who refused to sign the treaty. During the years that followed, there was some fighting between the Sioux and the whites. But Red Cloud and his people stayed in the wild Powder River hunting grounds. For them this was a good time. They kept up their old war with the Crows, and many warriors won honors in battle. The Bad Face band had a pleasant camp with other Oglala camps nearby. They hunted freely from the Big Horn Mountains to the Black Hills. In this country there were no white men to scare away the game.

The Oglalas called this the Time of Plenty Buffalo. In the evening Red Cloud walked through his camp. He was content with all he saw. There was meat in the cooking pots. Red Cloud's children played happily with their friends. The ponies grew fat on the rich grass.

A friendly trader had brought in supplies and settled nearby. The people could trade their furs and buffalo robes for iron to make arrowheads and for good blankets, coffee, and sugar. They had everything they wanted.

The Indian agent kept sending messengers to Red Cloud.

"Your people must stop fighting the Crows!" they told him. "Wars between Indians are dangerous for white people in the Plains country."

The agent also ordered Red Cloud to come to Fort Laramie and sign the treaty.

His orders only brought laughter from the Sioux.

6
A Trail Through the Wilderness

White men had been going to the gold diggings in Montana by a long hard trip along the Medicine Road and through a steep mountain pass. They wanted a shorter, easier way. They found such a way along the east side of the Big Horn Mountains. They marked a trail there.

Oglala hunters brought Red Cloud word of this trail through the finest Sioux hunting grounds. The chief was furious. He rode to the trail with some of his warriors.

As the Indians were studying the marks

made by iron-shod horses and wagon wheels, two white men rode around a bend. One of them was John Bozeman, the miner who had marked the trail. Red Cloud's warriors quickly surrounded the men.

"Drop your guns! Get off your horses!" Red Cloud ordered the frightened miners.

Red Cloud did not want trouble with the white men. He only wanted them to stay out of his country.

"I will let you go back to the Medicine Road," he told Bozeman. "But do not come here again."

To teach the white men a lesson, he had his warriors take their clothes. Naked and unarmed, they struggled back to Fort Laramie on foot.

Even after that, the whites kept on trying to use the Bozeman Trail. Some miners got through to Montana traveling by night and hiding by day. Others were attacked and killed by Sioux hunters. More travelers kept coming.

At last Red Cloud had signal fires lighted to summon a war party. Chief Red Leaf and his Wazhazas came in answer to signals flashed from the hills with mirrors. Several other bands came also. They rode swiftly to the Bozeman Trail.

It happened that some army wagons were rumbling up the trail. At sunset they were driven into a circle and supper fires were lighted.

Red Cloud and his warriors were watching from the hills. Red Cloud planned to frighten these soldiers and then drive them away with a warning. In the morning the soldiers awoke to see a silent ring of mounted warriors surrounding their camp. To the white men, the grim-faced Sioux looked like hungry wolves.

The soldiers opened fire on the Indians, but

they were too far away to hit anyone. The warriors sat there, waiting. Hours passed. The white men became more and more nervous. They were greatly outnumbered, so they did not dare to try to break through the circle of Indians.

When darkness came, Red Cloud had a ring of fires lighted around the wagon camp. They burned and twinkled in the dark wilderness night. There was not a sound from the Indians, but the soldiers knew that they were out in the shadows, waiting.

This went on for two weeks. From time to time soldiers tried to sneak out of camp. The warriors always drove them back. Red Cloud smiled when he saw that the soldiers' firewood had given out. Their food was low also.

The army men were frightened, and Red Cloud had worries of his own. His younger warriors were getting restless. War whoops rang out as they galloped their horses recklessly around the wagon camp. They wanted to ride in and kill every white man they could. Only their respect for Red Cloud held them back.

Finally Red Cloud decided to let two men sneak out of the camp. He sent scouts to trail them back to Fort Laramie. Soon the scouts reported back to Red Cloud. A large company of army men was coming to rescue the wagon train. The scouts had learned that the army officer at Laramie had ordered that the wagons be taken back to the Medicine Road. None of the whites were to try to go on up the Bozeman Trail.

This was what Red Cloud wanted. He withdrew his war party up the trail. If the wagons went back, he would let them go in peace. If they tried to go on, he would fight and wipe them out.

The soldiers from Fort Laramie made the wagons go back.

For a few months after that no white man dared enter the Powder River–Big Horn country. Then one day soldiers marched again into the Sioux hunting grounds. This time they came with many men and guns. It was clear that the government meant to take the Indians' land.

"The white man always wants a war," Red Cloud grumbled.

He had planned to go hunting. But if the soldiers wanted war, he would give them war!

Led by their greatest chiefs, Sioux warriors gathered to stop this new invasion. They made sudden whirlwind attacks on the white soldiers. They drove off army horses and captured supply wagons. Like angry hornets they chased the starving soldiers back to Fort Laramie.

The government had spent millions of dollars and lost many men. Still it had not crushed the Sioux. Now a new Indian agent was sent to Fort Laramie. He had strong orders to get all the Sioux chiefs to a peace council.

The agent sent out messengers. They promised the Sioux guns and other presents if they would come to the fort.

Red Cloud's warriors wanted guns. So the Bad Face band went to Laramie with the other Oglala bands. The agent met the chiefs inside a huge tent. He asked them to sign a treaty that would permit whites to travel on the Bozeman Trail.

Red Cloud rose from his place in the circle of dignified chiefs.

"The Powder River country is our last good hunting ground," he said sternly. "If white people come there, they will kill all the buffalo."

Just then an Indian slipped into the tent and whispered to Red Cloud. "Many soldiers have arrived. It is said that they come to build forts on the Bozeman Trail."

Red Cloud's eyes blazed with fury. "The Great Father in Washington treats us like children!" he shouted. "He sends us presents and asks for a road through our country. But before we can say yes or no, he sends the army to steal the road."

The tent was as still as the prairie before a great storm.

"The white men have broken every treaty they have made with us," Red Cloud continued scornfully. "We will sign no new treaty. And I will fight to keep white intruders out of our hunting grounds." He held his rifle high. "Brave hearts, follow me!"

He strode from the tent and the other chiefs followed.

Within a short time the Sioux were headed back to the Powder River country.

The government was determined to use soldiers to build a road and forts in the Sioux hunting grounds. Red Cloud sent a warning that any whites who entered the Powder River country would be killed. But the Indian agent reported to the government that Red Cloud was not an important chief. "The army can easily push him aside," the agent insisted.

And so, in the summer of 1866, Colonel Carrington and his soldiers set out for the Bozeman Trail. When this news reached Red Cloud, the many bands of the Sioux were scattered on buffalo hunts. Red Cloud called them together again. Some friendly Cheyenne Indians came also. They gathered on Little Goose Creek in the Powder River country. Their tepees were so many that they stretched for miles along the stream.

7
Red Cloud's War

The big Sioux camp on Little Goose Creek hummed with the news brought from the Bozeman Trail by Red Cloud's scouts. Colonel Carrington had built a fort at the foot of the Big Horn Mountains!

"This fort is an insult to us, as well as a threat," Red Cloud said in the council of chiefs. "Brothers, I am for war!"

Thousands of warriors from the different bands of the Sioux were ready and eager to follow Red Cloud into battle. As war chief of the entire Sioux Nation, his power was greater than ever before.

The new army post was called Fort Phil

Kearney. Two other forts were built on the Bozeman Trail. Red Cloud sent warriors to attack the smaller forts, but he kept most of his force near Fort Phil Kearney.

Fear of the big cannon on the walls of the fort kept the warriors from hurling themselves against the log walls. But they kept a sharp watch on the fort and no one could get in or out without a bitter fight. Sometimes warriors crept up very close to kill sentries and drive off army horses and mules.

Every time woodcutters went out with wagons to cut and haul wood, they were attacked. Few supply wagons were able to reach the fort. Only well-guarded army trains dared to travel the Bozeman Trail. Even then many soldiers were killed by the swift-circling warriors.

Captain Fetterman, a young officer at the fort, had great scorn for Indians.

"Give me 80 men and I'll ride through the entire Sioux Nation!" he boasted.

Another officer vowed to kill Red Cloud.

On a cold morning in December, they had their chance to meet Red Cloud and his warriors. Some woodcutters were attacked on the trail by a small number of Indians. Captain Fetterman set out with 80 men to rescue them.

Red Cloud had a war party hidden on the wooded slopes above the trail. When Captain Fetterman appeared, the Indians who had been fighting the woodcutters pretended to run away. The captain and his men rushed after them. The warriors fled across a little stream. The soldiers started to follow. Then suddenly the woods was full of Sioux and Cheyenne warriors. From every side they rushed at Fetterman and his men. The soldiers fought bravely, but every one of them was killed.

The next day a blizzard swept over the Big Horn country. It was the beginning of a long hard winter. The Indians could not move about freely in the deep snow. But Red Cloud kept his warriors together. And he kept the Bozeman Trail closed.

When summer came a teamster managed to reach Fort Phil Kearney with a new kind of fast-loading rifle.

Armed with the new guns, a company of soldiers and woodcutters went up the trail. Red Cloud attacked them with a war party.

The Indians did not know about the deadly new rifles. Most of the warriors carried only bows and arrows. Once it had been possible for a skilled bowman to shoot several arrows in the time it took a soldier to load and shoot his gun only once. But with the new rifles, the soldiers could keep up a constant, terrible fire that stopped the warriors again and again.

"It's a good day to die!" shouted the Sioux as they attacked the soldiers again and again. Bullets from the rapid-firing rifles mowed the Indians down. Waves of warriors kept coming. The bitter fight went on all day.

Suddenly Red Cloud saw a company of soldiers coming from the fort. They had one of the cannon from the fort. The cannon boomed and a shell scattered a group of warriors.

Indian bowmen were helpless before this big gun. Red Cloud called his warriors back.

The soldiers remembered what had happened to Captain Fetterman and they did not pursue the Indians. With the woodcutters, they fell back to Fort Phil Kearney.

Red Cloud continued his war. For another year he kept up the attacks on the forts on the Bozeman Trail. At last the government came to understand that he was indeed a powerful chief and that he would never give in. The Indian agent was ordered to invite him, and some other leading chiefs, to another peace council.

Red Cloud sent word that when the last soldier left his country, he would see about a peace treaty.

8

As Long As Grass Shall Grow

The army could not defeat Red Cloud because they did not have enough soldiers. Also, many people back east were demanding that this war must stop. The army and the agent knew that the Sioux would not accept any treaty that did not bear Red Cloud's name. So they gave in to his demands.

It was a proud day for the Sioux Nation when the flag was lowered at Fort Phil Kearney. The sad, silvery notes of a bugle floated over the hills. Then the soldiers marched out of the fort and away down the Bozeman Trail.

Before the soldiers were out of sight, Red Cloud's warriors rode into the fort. Soon a great cloud of fire and smoke rolled up into the sky. Fort Phil Kearney was burning to the ground!

The Sioux destroyed the other two forts also.

Red Cloud believed that he had saved the Sioux hunting grounds. As the proud chief of a great nation, he led his people to Fort Laramie. The agent read the new treaty to him. It seemed fair to Red Cloud, and he signed it in good faith.

This Treaty of 1868 was the most famous treaty ever made between the Indians and the government. It made the entire present state of South Dakota into a reservation for the Sioux. This meant that this territory would be "reserved" forever for the Indians. The government hoped that all the Sioux would go to live on the reservation.

The Powder River country was to be kept by the Sioux for hunting grounds. The treaty promised that this land would belong to the Sioux for "as long as grass shall grow and water flow." All white people were forbidden to enter Powder River country. But the Sioux could leave the reservation to hunt there whenever they wished to do so.

The Sioux gave some land to the government. And they agreed to let the white men build a railroad across the plains. In return, the treaty promised the Indians payments of food, clothing, and money. Red Cloud promised never to fight the white men again.

The government appointed Indian agents to live with the Sioux. The part of the reservation where an agent's house was built was called an agency. Here storehouses were built also. They held the goods that were to be paid to the Indians for the land they had given the government. One agency was called Red Cloud in honor of the great Oglala chief. Another agency, not far away, was called Spotted Tail for the head chief of the Brulé Sioux.

The treaty promised that schools for Sioux children would be built at the agencies. Their parents were to be given tools and helped to become farmers.

The agent kept urging Red Cloud to live on the reservation. He did live there during the winters. But in summer he and most of his people returned to their beloved hunting grounds.

Red Cloud kept honestly to the Treaty of 1868. But he did not want his people to become like white men. Some day the Sioux might have to become farmers and "scratch the earth." They might have to raise cattle for food, instead of hunting buffalo and other wild game. But he wanted them to cling to the old free life as long as possible. And they must always remain true to the laws and beliefs of the Seven Council Fires.

The agent at the Red Cloud Agency complained bitterly to the government in Washington. "Red Cloud will not let the Sioux learn to live like white people," he wrote.

The government had another cause for worry. White people wanted to settle in Wyoming near the Powder River country. This might stir the Sioux to fight another war.

The president invited Red Cloud to Washington to talk about these matters.

Red Cloud and some other chiefs traveled to Washington on the train. It was a strange new experience for them to ride on an "iron horse." In Washington President Grant gave a grand banquet to welcome them.

All of the most important people in Washington gathered at the White House. The East Room was noisy with their talk and laughter as they waited to meet the visiting chiefs. Then Red Cloud appeared in the doorway. Everyone fell silent at the sight of this magnificent man.

Red Cloud towered over the tallest man present. A splendid buffalo robe, decorated with wide bands of quillwork, was flung over his shoulder. He wore a deerskin shirt embroidered with colorful designs and deeply fringed. His red leggings were richly worked with quills and beads. In his long, glossy black hair he wore a single eagle feather. As he strode into the room, a murmur of admiration rose from the other guests.

Red Cloud replied to the president's welcome with great dignity and politeness. Nellie, the president's little daughter,

stepped up to him. She made a curtsy and handed him a lovely bouquet of flowers.

Red Cloud smiled kindly at Nellie and thanked her in his soft Sioux speech. Then he sighed as he thought longingly of his own daughter Lucy so far away.

The next day the chiefs were taken to the navy yard to watch some cannon being fired. Red Cloud noted that these were dangerous guns indeed.

By this time he knew that the people of the United States were as many as blades of grass in summer. And their wealth and power were beyond belief! This knowledge did not break his spirit, as the government hoped it would. He spoke strongly to the president and his "council."

"The whites are not keeping to the terms of the treaty between us. You want peace. Let your people keep their feet from Indian trails and there will be peace!"

He did not trust these white people. He longed to return home.

"My heart is with my people," he said in a voice deep with feeling. "I think of them sleeping and waking, for they are always on my heart."

In spite of the honors paid him in Washington, he was glad to get back to the reservation. In the spring he moved his band back to Powder River. Many other Sioux joined them. This was the free life that Red Cloud loved. The hunting was good. There were dances and feasts. Sometimes a war party went out against the Crows.

Red Cloud's eldest son, a brave young warrior, was killed in battle with the Crows. Red Cloud and We-tamahech mourned him deeply, and Red Cloud gave away many horses in his memory.

There were still two sons and a pretty

young daughter to bring cheer to the chief's tepee.

Often in the evening, Red Leaf and other friends came to smoke at Red Cloud's fire. It was like the good days before the white men came.

In wintertime Red Cloud's band returned to the reservation. One winter they met bad news. Gold, the yellow stone that drove white people crazy, had been found in the Black Hills. Now hundreds of white miners were pouring into Pa Sapa. Sioux warriors were demanding that their chiefs drive the invaders away.

The Indian agent warned the government that the Sioux were talking of war. In reply, an invitation came for Red Cloud to visit the president again. They would talk about this new trouble.

9
The Black Hills

In Washington Red Cloud met Spotted Tail and some other Sioux chiefs. They exchanged worried glances. Why had the Great Father brought them together? They soon found out. The president told them that the government wanted to buy the Black Hills.

"If you refuse to sell," he said, "we will take them by force."

The chiefs were stunned by this bad news that had come to them.

"We will never sell Pa Sapa," Red Cloud said firmly. "The Black Hills are part of the land that is to belong to us 'as long as grass shall grow.' Does any white man in Washington remember this?"

The chiefs returned home and met with all the tribes of the Sioux Nation in a great council. Government agents came also.

"Name your price for the Black Hills," they said.

To a Sioux the Black Hills were priceless.

"Let us end this matter by asking a price too high for the Great Father to pay," Red Cloud said to the other chiefs.

"We want six hundred million dollars," he told the agents. They glared at him.

"The government must also feed and clothe my people for seven generations," Red Cloud continued calmly. "And every family must have a wagon, and a team of horses, and a cow, and pigs, and chickens. And I want some good white man's houses built for my people!"

His eyes flashed. "You are stealing our

hunting grounds. Soon we must become farmers or starve. We do not wish to be like white people. If you insist on making white people of us, you must pay the bill!"

The angry agents returned to Washington and reported that the Black Hills must be taken by force. The army moved at once into Sioux lands. Many Sioux warriors went on the warpath against the hated soldiers.

Red Cloud took no part in this war. He had promised not to fight the soldiers again. Not only that, he had seen the power of the United States. He knew that his people could not win another war against the white men. It would be better to fight them in council, instead of in battle. But his heart was with the warrior bands. He longed to be with them. When his son Jack went to join the fighting Sioux, Red Cloud gave him his precious silver-mounted rifle.

One day in June 1876, a great Sioux and Cheyenne war party wiped out an entire regiment of soldiers. White men called this Indian victory the Battle of the Little Bighorn.

After the great battle the Sioux bands scattered, instead of staying together as in Red Cloud's War. This made it possible for the army to defeat them one by one.

The army also moved troops onto the reservation and took over the agency. Red Cloud protested angrily. Many of the Sioux had taken no part in the war. Yet now they were being punished by the army. No new supplies were sent to the agency. There was not enough food to feed the people. And with the soldiers moving about, the game was frightened away. Yet the soldiers would not let the Indians leave the agency to hunt in the wild lands.

Red Cloud complained to the army

officer who was now in command on the reservation. "My people are not getting enough to eat. Food was promised us in payment for the land on which the iron horse was built. Where is this food?"

Other chiefs and headmen joined in his complaints.

The officer glared at the angry chiefs. "Your people will soon get nothing at all to eat unless you sign a paper giving us the Black Hills. Also, we will force the entire Sioux Nation to move to Indian Territory in Oklahoma."

"You cannot do this!" Red Cloud shouted. "My people would die in that hot country."

"Then touch the pen and give us the Black Hills!"

But Red Cloud and the other chiefs could not bring themselves to sign away Pa Sapa. Their defiance made the officer angrier than ever. He cut off all food supplies to the Sioux. It tore Red Cloud's heart to see his people starving. Old people were growing more feeble. He heard children crying for food. Sick people were dying for lack of nourishment.

The gaunt and worried chiefs held a council to decide what they should do. Surely it would be better to lose Pa Sapa than to see their people die of hunger. And even worse than death to the Sioux was the threat that they would be driven away from their homeland forever.

With heavy hearts Red Cloud and the other chiefs touched the pen to save their hungry people.

Now that the government had forced the Sioux to give away the Black Hills, the soldiers opened the storehouses. But the food they handed out was poor and scanty. In vain Red Cloud demanded more and better supplies for all his people. The commanding officer was still angry with him because he had held out so long against the government. He threatened to throw Red Cloud and some other chiefs into jail.

To escape from the unpleasant life at the Red Cloud Agency, Red Cloud and Red Leaf moved their bands some distance away. They camped in wild, lonely country, far from the hated soldiers. Here there was still deer and other game, and the hunters could provide meat for the cooking pots.

The army commander was furious because Red Cloud had moved away.

One cold morning Red Cloud awoke to a feeling of danger. He took up his rifle and pulled aside the robe that covered the door of the tepee. He found himself looking straight at a soldier armed with a rifle.

Led by Pawnee scouts, the soldiers had tracked the two chiefs to this peaceful camp. They had surrounded the tepees.

"Lay down your gun, Red Cloud, or we will fire into the tepees!" shouted the officer in charge of the soldiers.

This meant that women and children would be hurt or killed. Red Cloud was boiling with rage. But for the sake of the helpless ones, he gave up his rifle. So did the other warriors.

The Pawnees were old enemies of the Sioux. They gleefully took away all the horses. We-tamahech's prized white chickens, of which she was very proud, were killed.

Red Cloud, the most magnificent horseman of the plains, was forced to walk back to the agency with a gun at his back. Red Leaf strode beside him. Their people, strung out in the rear, were threatened by the guns of the soldiers. It seemed like the end of the world to the two proud chiefs.

Back at the agency, Red Cloud stood tall before the commanding officer. "This is a very bad thing that you have done," he said. "My camp was peaceful, and we have the right to hunt on our own lands. The Great Father told me so. He told me years ago, when I untied my pony's tail and promised not to fight again."

"Times have changed," the officer said, frowning. "Red Cloud, you are too proud. You encourage your people to defy the government. The Great Father is removing you from your place as head chief of the Sioux. Spotted Tail will now be chief."

This did not trouble Red Cloud as much as the officer thought it would. Let them set up a new head chief! Most of the Oglalas would still look upon Red Cloud as their leader.

In time the government realized that this was true. If it wanted peace with the Sioux, it must have Red Cloud's good will.

It was decided to move the Red Cloud

Agency farther north. Red Cloud and his people chose the place. At Pine Ridge they would live within sight of the Black Hills. The government built a comfortable house there for Red Cloud. And he was given a good income to make up for all the horses stolen by the Pawnees and the soldiers.

For We-tamahech there was an iron cookstove, a rocking chair, and a sewing machine. And the agent found her a new flock of white chickens. Red Cloud's finest horse was kept tied at the door, ready for the chief to ride out to hunt.

Red Cloud lived to be a very old man. His eyes grew dim, but his back was as straight as ever. The Sioux still talked about his great deeds. White Americans came to see him and made much of him. Red Cloud was always dignified and courteous. But his heart was sad for the great, lost days of the Sioux Nation.